BRANCH LINES TO LONGMOOR

Vic Mitchell and Keith Smith

INTRODUCTION

This volume is intended to be a visual record of the line and to give an impression of some of the varied equipment that has been used on it, together with some of the special events that have taken place.

Space precludes detailed accounts of locomotive transfers or any record of the military units involved with the line. Much of this information is recorded in Ronald and Carter's *Longmoor Military Railway* (David & Charles 1974), together with many other historical facts.

There are many discrepancies to be found in the records from the past. Dates vary from what actually happened in the field; to when it was officially approved, and to when it was locally authorised. Sometimes events occurred in the reverse order of normal practice! With a track laying machine with a capability of one mile per day, accurate records of track layouts are impossible. We therefore apologise in advance for any apparent inconsistencies.

Other views of the line and the railways of the area are to be found in Peter Hay's *Steaming through East Hants.* (Middleton Press)

ISBN 0 906520 41 X

Design – Deborah Goodridge

First published June 1987

© *Middleton Press, 1987*

Typeset by CitySet - Bosham 573270

Published by Middleton Press
        Easebourne Lane
        Midhurst, West Sussex
        GU29 9AZ
        ☎ *073 081 3169*

Printed & bound by Biddles Ltd,
        Guildford and Kings Lynn

CONTENTS

ACKNOWLEDGEMENTS

We are very grateful to those whose names appear in the photograph credits and to Mrs. E. Fisk, K. Catchpole, D. Cullum, C.R. Gordon Stuart, Dr. T.A. Gough, R. Randell, Col. D.W. Ronald, Major J.A. Robins and N. Stanyon. As always, our wives have been of great assistance.

GEOGRAPHICAL SETTING

The entire route traverses the western extremity of the Lower Greensand, much of it on the infertile Sandgate Beds. The altitude is 200-300ft above sea level and the area is poorly drained, being at the watershed of the Rivers Wey and Rother.

Apart from a mile at the south end, the line was built on Crown land. Woolmer Forest had been a royal hunting ground and, like the New Forest, lost many of its trees in medieval times for fuel, building and manufacturing purposes.

The resulting barren land was extensively taken over by the Army, in the late nineteenth century, for training purposes. Much of it has now returned to nature, although concealed explosives form an unnatural hazard and preclude indiscriminant rambling.

The natural history of the area was studied by Gilbert White of Selborne in the eighteenth century, it leading him to publish a book which was to become the foundation of the science of botany.

All maps are to the scale of 25" to 1 mile, unless otherwise stated.

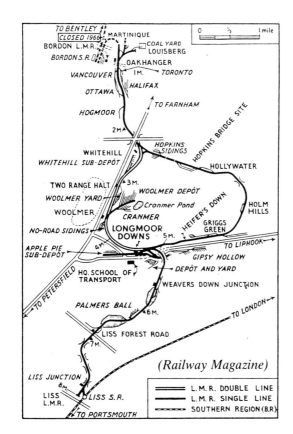

(Railway Magazine)

HISTORICAL BACKGROUND

A hutted camp was constructed at Longmoor in 1900-03 but because of complaints of bad ground conditions in winter, 68 huts were moved to Bordon in 1903. Royal Engineers were given this task. At the same time, plans were being made for the construction of a military training railway in the area. Some details of the hut moving operation are worth quoting. Each hut was 72 x 21ft and weighed over 30 tons. Two 18″ gauge tracks were laid, 14ft apart and the huts jacked up onto 14 bogies. Propulsion was achieved by use of a steam-powered rail-mounted winch, which was secured to suitable trees by means of steel rope. Repeating the operation every 400yds, four huts per day were moved along the 4½ mile route.

The Bordon and Longmoor Military Railway was authorised in 1906 although construction had started in the previous year. Materials arrived from the store at Woolwich via the LSWR branch to Bordon, which opened to passengers on 11th December 1905.

In 1908, it was designated the Woolmer Instructional Military Railway, a name which was used until 1935, when it became the Longmoor Military Railway. In 1912 agreement was made for the movement of LSWR coaches on troop trains over the line.

Expansion and contraction of the facilities has taken place as military and political circumstances have changed over the years. Peaks of activity occurred during the World Wars, notably in 1944. Construction of the extension to Liss started in August 1924 and the line was brought into full use in August 1933, although the rail connection to the main line was not made until 1942.

The BR branch to Bordon closed on 4th April 1966 and soon after that the LMR operation was cut back to Oakhanger. (The branch passenger services had ceased in 1957).

Official closure of the remainder of the line took place on 31st October 1969 although some movements took place in 1970 in connection with the proposed Longmoor Steam Railway. 1½ miles of track at the Liss end were leased for this purpose but the scheme was unsuccessful and the last vehicles had gone by October 1971.

PASSENGER SERVICES

Travel was restricted to servicemen, service families and civilian employees, other than on the public open days.

Initially, the service was on an "as required" basis but by the early 1930s a regular time-table of about four trains per day was being operated. By 1939, up to 50 passengers per day were being carried but with the rapid expansion of the camps and stores in the area in the early part of WWII, the figure increased to over 3000 daily. There were often over twenty passenger trains each way.

After the war, a slow decline in frequency of service took place, until by the mid-1960s there were only four journeys north of Long-moor and nine to Liss. These timetabled trains were known as *The Bullet.*

1. The mobile winch, seen in front of one of the huts it was moving, was inadequate on the steeply graded part of the route, near Whitehill. The rope from the winding drum under the boiler of this Fowler ploughing engine was pulled out manually to assist passage over the high ground. The engine has a horizontal steering wheel and a steam dome – features not to be found on 20th century models. (Museum of Army Transport)

2. Armies in retreat need to disrupt communications for their pursuers. A track wrecker which broke every sleeper in its path was ideal. Explosives could be used additionally, to bend the rails. This example was captured in Italy and was an historic exhibit at Longmoor for many years, now being in the Museum of Army Transport.
(G.M. Moon)

. Like most military installations, the terminus was very smart in appearance – note the initial letters of the railway on the grass bank. This 1934 view shows 2–4–2T *Earl* *Roberts*, having received the signal to reverse from the lower semaphore arm. (E.R. Lacey collection)

4. Another view north shows the central goods exchange platform and, on the left, the SR signal box and water tank. Their locomotive shed is in the middle of the picture – the WIMR had earlier had a shed behind the cottages. (Museum of Army Transport)

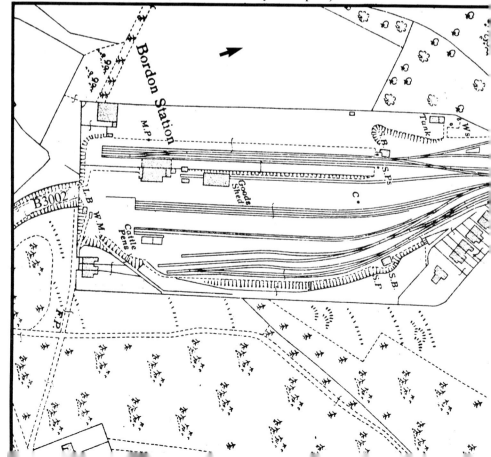

5. On the left is the WIMR platform and block post. The Army preferred this description of a signal box and so it will be used throughout this album. When the tracks were expanded in 1916, the former LSWR cottages seen in the previous pictures lost a large part of their gardens and subsequently the only means of access to them was by way of the foot crossing seen here. (Museum of Army Transport)

The 1936 survey shows the SR lines at the top and the LMR at the bottom. Initially, military trains terminated in the field behind the cottages, although an exchange siding was provided from the outset.

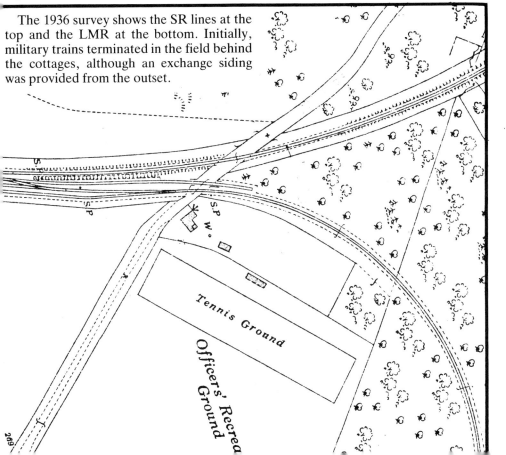

Tennis Ground

Officers' Recrea Ground

269

6. During the early part of WWII, the sidings here became extremely congested. The two exchange sidings only held 15 wagons each and had to be cleared up to six times a day. One locomotive involved in this hectic work was ex-LNER class J69 no. 7088.
(H.N. James)

7. A 1946 photograph shows this Vulcan Foundry product when only a year old. It was later renumbered WD181 and remained on the LMR until 1959. The coaches are the "Blue Saloons", the rear one of which is shown in more detail in picture no.87.
(J.G. Sturt)

8. On 4th October 1958, a railway enthusiasts' special ran from Waterloo via Effingham Junction to Liss for a journey over the LMR. It is seen at the goods exchange platform, prior to returning to London via Aldershot. Nearly 30 years later, the locomotive was again to be found in steam in East Hampshire – on the "Watercress Line". (S.C. Nash)

9. A photograph from January 1966 shows no. AD102 almost at the southern end of the station site. The military tracks had been extended south, to the boundary fence shown on the map. The map also shows the B3002 terminating at the white gates seen in this view. (D. Fereday Glenn)

10. In March 1970, the notice still read – *"CIVILIANS EXCEPT WAR DEPARTMENT EMPLOYEES ON DUTY OR PROCEEDING TO OR FROM THEIR WORK MAY NOT TRAVEL. SOLDIERS NOT ON DUTY THEIR WIVES AND FAMILIES AND WAR DEPART-MENT EMPLOYEES MAY TRAVEL AT THEIR OWN RISK."*

The site is now occupied by a bustling industrial estate. Views of the SR station will appear in a future album. (J.H. Bird)

11. Looking north in about 1932, we see the SR single line from Bentley on the left, with the new signals awaiting their arms. The signal at "off" is for the WIMR line on the right. An independent, parallel goods line ran as far as Oakhanger during the peak traffic era of the LMR. (Museum of Army Transport)

12. A closer look at the level crossing, seen in the background of the previous picture, shows that the exchange siding no longer crossed the road. This picture was taken from a train bound for Bentley on 9th January 1966. On the right, the LMR starts on a semi-circular course to reach Oakhanger and its southerly route to Longmoor. (G.M. Moon)

OAKHANGER

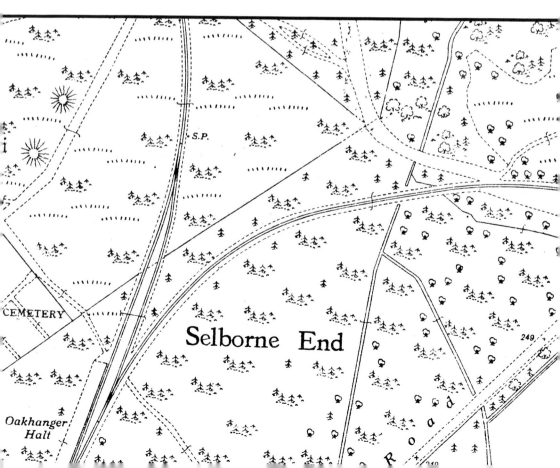

13. Training was given in all aspects of railway operation, including the use of diesel locomotives, which were still uncommon in WWII. This is LMS no. 7098. The lettered discs indicated daily duty rosters but by 1944 there were more than 26 and so shunting duties were unlettered. (H.N. James)

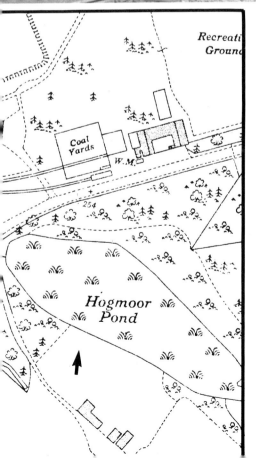

14. This is one of a very large number of American built tanks to have worked briefly on the LMR in the latter part of WWII, prior to shipment to Europe. The load of timber is a reminder of the vast tonnage of such material that was carried on the line in the previous World War. This was in connection with a saw mill set up by the Canadian Army. (H.N. James)

Described as Oakhanger Halt in the 1936 survey, it was regarded as the station for Bordon Garrison. The branch shown was used for coal and supplies to the Louisburg Barracks and was known as the Louisburg branch.

←———

15. 2–10–0 no. 600 *Gordon* heads the last train on 31st October 1969. In September 1971, this locomotive was moved to the Severn Valley Railway where its bright blue livery and white wheels have continued to draw the admiring crowds. (J. Scrace)

←———

16. Two photographs, taken six months after closure, show the buffer stops which had been placed on the second track after WWII, as the MOT had objected to a *double track* ungated road crossing. Trouble had earlier arisen when the local authority objected to the Army's *unauthorised* crossing of the highway, prior to WWI. (J.H. Bird)

17. The sixteen lever frame included a four-lever brass section added after the main frame was built in 1951 and is now an exhibit at the Museum of Army Transport. The line curving to the left was to Toronto sidings. (J.H. Bird)

18. Ex-LSWR class 02 no. 213 came to grief in Toronto sidings in November 1943, due to over running signals. It was one of the first engines on the line to use vacuum brakes and was returned to the SR, badly battered but not beyond repair.
(Museum of Army Transport)

19. Initially the line crossed the Farnham Petersfield road on the level and during th hut moving operation, one of them becam derailed and was abandoned. It is seen he serving as the local police station, the ma road being in the foreground and two e Kent & East Sussex coaches in th background. (Lens of Sutton)

20. Eventually the standard gauge line was carried under the main road, at the cross roads with the Standford and Blackmoor turnings. Hawthorn Leslie 0–6–0T *Selborne* is seen from the bridge, bound for Bordon on 5th April 1938. It was fitted with a chime whistle, more common on express locomotives, and was built specially for the WIMR. (National Railway Museum)

WHITEHILL

21. The timber platform was on the up side, south of the bridge. This 0–6–2T was earlier Taff Vale Railway no.28 and is now restored to that livery. It belongs to the National Museum of Wales, having been built in Cardiff in 1897. It was the first Army locomotive to bear the name *Gordon*. (H.N. James)

22. A soutbound train stands by Whitehi block post, headed by SR class D1 no. 223. Three of these 0–4–2Ts were hired in 194. 44 but no. 2233 ended its career in the eart buffer stops at Liss Forest Road. It was hau ing a train of "brass hats" who had dined Longmoor, shortly before D-Day. (H.N. James)

23. 0–6–2T *Sir John French* and SR 0–4–4T no. 213 ease empty bogie bolsters north, in about 1942. At that time very extensive military stores were being built alongside the railway, necessitating double track between Whitehill and Longmoor from 1943 onwards. (H.N. James)

24. In May 1949, the first of many film companies arrived to use the line as a set. The film was the "Interrupted Journey", starring Valerie Hobson and Richard Todd. Two of the old Army ambulances were painted in GWR colours – on the camera side only! (A.G.W. Garraway)

HOLLYWATER LOOP

26. The loop left the main line at a triangular junction at Whitehill and rejoined it at Longmoor. It was fully operational from 1942 until 1968, this being the first visit of the inspection saloon no. 111 (ex-Kent & East Sussex Railway) on 29th June 1942. The locomotive is ex-LSWR class 02 no. 213. (H.N. James)

25. Much of the filming was done at night with Dean Goods no. WD70195 in the lead and many Sappers as extras. Further details of this event and other happenings on military railways are to be found in *Garraway, Father & Son*, published by Middleton Press. (A.G.W. Garraway)

27. The loop gave the opportunity for continuous running of various types of trains on a route that had both single and double track, varied signalling and numerous sidings. Class D1 no. 2240 is at the head of a 14-wagon train which worked a 24-hour service as a "crash" training course for civilian railwaymen. (H.N. James)

28. Class D1 0–4–2T no. 2286 ran away in the long siding parallel to the Liphook Road and produced an unscheduled rerailing exercise for wartime students. The loop was frequently lifted and relaid, for practice. (H.N. James)

During the Second World War, the maximum track mileage at Longmoor was about 70 and the manpower rose from about 500 in 1939 to 2,325 in 1942; there was also an annual turnover of 27,000 trainees. The peak traffic year was 1944, when almost 602,000 tons of traffic were exchanged with the Southern Railway. At one time 27 engines were in steam, 850 wagons were exchanged in one day and the highest passenger figure for one day was 7,687.

The workshops were also very busy. As well as preparing and despatching over 700 locomotives overseas, a great variety of experimental work was undertaken on the loading of locomotives on transporters and craft, in the design and manufacture of slinging gear and securing tackles, the building of steel bridges for the Rhine ferries and the assembly and trial of mobile refrigerators for the Far East.

ARMÉE BRITANNIQUE.

$\dfrac{\text{Exemplaire}}{\text{Copy}}$ No. **2**

BON DE CHEMIN DE FER

General Railway Warrant

Pour le Transport a Exécuter par train
For the movement by _____ *No 2* _____ train.

De _____ à
From ____ *Hollywater* ____ to ____ *Woolmer*

Par _____ d'un Détachement.
Via _____ of a party.

Commandé par _____
Under the command of ____ *Sergr Weaver*

9. It was not all continuous running on the Hollywater Loop. The much battered Dean Goods 0–6–0 was often used for rerailing exercises, as seen here at Griggs Green on the Liphook Road on 24th June 1953. (A.G.W. Garraway)

30. There was a passing loop at Hollywater and a platform was erected there in later years simply for crews to practise stopping. The loop was severed in 1968 for culvert repairs and never reinstated. (Museum of Army Transport)

31. This 1938 dual-braked Bagnall 0–6–2T, the second locomotive to be named *Kitchener*, is seen from the block post during WWII, as the single line tablet is about to be surrendered. It was named after Lord Kitchener, a former RE officer. (H.N. James)

32. A later photograph from the same viewpoint shows part of the extensive array of sidings provided in this area, prior to the doubling of the main line. The LMR locomotive is ex-LBSCR class I2 4–4–2T, named by the Army *Earl Roberts*, after the war. (R.C. Riley)

33. A photograph taken shortly after the closure of the line shows details of the block post, which was located three miles from Bordon, close to the A325 road and its turning to Blackmoor. The frame contained ten levers. (Museum of Army Transport)

34. Ex-LNER class J69s were acquired at the outbreak of WWII to supplement the three serviceable LMR engines. No. 7344 had its previous owner's initials painted over and was eventually given a WD number (88). The block post on the left had 10 levers in 1936 and the signal is one of the original lower quadrant type. (H.N. James)

35. Another WWII photograph shows WD no. 1255, described as the first of the USA built 0–6–0Ts to go into use on the LMR. Part of the expanding network of sidings is to be seen, as is the RE badge in the centre of the smokebox door. (H.N. James)

6. The extensive wartime stores are obscured by SR class A12 no. 625 and its train. Three Adams Jubilees were hired by the LMR in 1940-43, this one being given the unofficial name of *The Emerald Queen* while on the line, owing to it having retained its SR malachite green livery. (H.N. James)

37. A southward view of the station from the Drewry railcar in June 1948 shows some of the eight reception sidings. At its zenith, there were over 40 other sidings in this area. Many of the black sheds housed locomotive parts. (S.W. Baker)

39. An undated photograph shows the basi
conditions prevailing in the early years. Th
platform, railway and public road wer
unfenced, allowing local childen an unintei
rupted view. (Lens of Sutton)

38. The final new locomotive was delivered
to the LMR in 1964. It was the diesel-
hydraulic 0–8–0 *General Lord Robertson*
from Rolls Royce Sentinel and is seen on its
way to Longmoor Downs on the public open
day held on 8th June 1968. It has subsequently worked for a time on the nearby Mid-
Hants Railway. (S.C. Nash)

→

40. A crude sleeper built platform allowed
easy loading of an even cruder troop train,
three vehicles of which had apparently been
borrowed from the Midland Railway. No
fatalities from rough shunting appear to have
been recorded. (Lens of Sutton)

41. The line was never short of variety in its locomotive fleet. LSWR class O415 4–4–2T no. 424 was in use from 1914 and in 1920 it was sent to Swindon Works for overhaul. It was there that it acquired the GWR-style safety valve cover. (G.M. Moon collection)

The 1910 map of 6″ scale shows the sta[n]dard gauge line from Bordon at the top. Th[e] line marked *TRAMWAY* was of 18″ gauge. Those between the parade ground and th[e] sewage works were either mixed gauge o[r] exchange sidings.

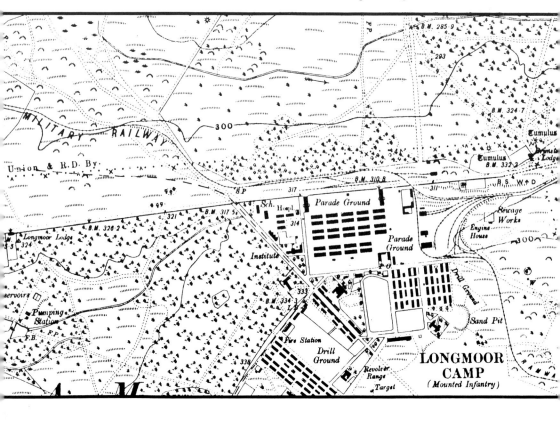

42. A 1932 eastward view shows a goods train bound for the line under construction to Liss and a passenger train having just crossed the Greatham-Liphook road, on its way from Longmoor Yard.
(Museum of Army Transport)

43. A programme of dramatic improvements had been started by 1923. This included provision of heavier rail (75lb/yd), new water tanks and solid ash-surfaced platforms. The latter items are visible in this photograph of Hawthorn Leslie 0–6–0T *Selborne*, taken on 17th May 1934. (H.C. Casserley)

44. The track layout at the west end of the station is evident as a passenger train departs for Bordon. Many of these trains ran empty and the platforms were often deserted during the middle of the day – training and experience was the objective.
(Museum of Army Transport)

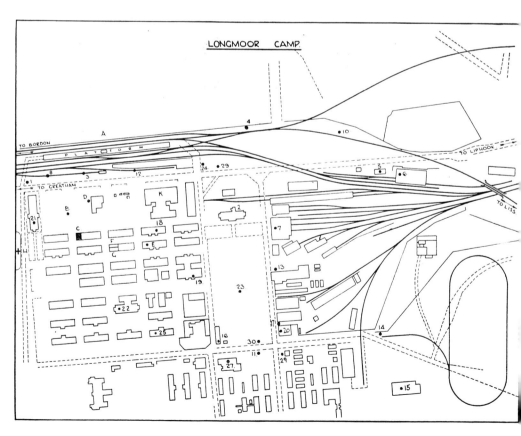

45. Typical military traffic is illustrated here, the bogie wagons with upturned ends being designated *RECTANKS*. The ones on the left are ex-GWR *MACAWS*. The white swastikas indicated enemy equipment during practice manoeuvres.
(Museum of Army Transport)

LOCATION OF PUBLIC DAY ATTRACTIONS

giving times of Demonstrations, etc.

3rd September 1955

A. LONGMOOR DOWNS STATION	D. ENQUIRIES & LOST PROPERTY	G. GENT'S CLOAK ROOM
B. CAR PARK	E. REST ROOM	H. FIRST AID POST
C. CYCLE STORE	F. LADIES' CLOAK ROOM	K. TEAS

1. Locomotive Ride Booking Office (Also See 24)
2. Transportation Centre Headquarters Building
3. Ramp Wagon Demonstration (**1.30, 3.30 and 5.15 p.m.**)
4. Breakdown Crane Re-railing locomotive (**2.00, 4.00 and 5.40 p.m.**)
5. Signal School
6. Diesel Locomotive shed
7. Locomotive Running shed
8. Pre-fabricated tracklaying demonstration (**2.30, 4.30 and 6.00 p.m.**)
10. Specimen tracks
11. Marine Exhibition
12. Railway Mobile Workshops
13. Competitions
14. Engineer Plant Exhibition. Miniature Railway Terminus
15. Radio Controlled Tank Demonstration (**2.20, 3.10, 3.50, 5.20 and 6.00 p.m.**)
16. Army Emergency Reserve Stand
17. Diving Display (**2.00, 2.45, 3.30, 4.15, 5.00 and 5.45 p.m.**)
18. Movement Control Model Room
19. Transportation Construction Model Room
20. Transportation Museum. Rail Wrecker
21. Garrison Church
22. Cookhouse and Dining Room
23. Drill Display (**2.30, 4.30 and 6.10 p.m.**) R.E. Band (**1.30, 3.00 and 5.00 p.m.**) Beating " Retreat " (**6.30 p.m.**)
24. Hollywater Trip (**2.40 and 5.10 p.m.**) and Locomotive Rides Ticket Office.
25. Barrack Room
27. Royal Engineers' Association. Regular Army Recruiter
29. Ice-Cream Stall
30. Fork-Lift Truck Rides

46. In the mid-1920s two wooden block posts were erected – East controlled the yard entrance and road crossing and West was situated on the main platform. The latter is seen here, after having been elevated in 1941 to facilitate the passage of troops marching on the platform. On the left is St. Martins Garrison Church and in the foreground can be seen the continental style method of point operation, using two wires instead of a rod. (Museum of Army Transport)

47. The church contained four notable stained glass windows donated by the four main railway companies. The entire structure has been dismantled and rebuilt at Leconfield, South Humberside. The lights are attached to spoked railway wagon wheels. (K. Catchpole)

48. In 1936, the LMR purchased this 62HP diesel-engined Drewry railcar. It was very successful despite being only single axle drive and was photographed on 5th June 1948, along with the new brick and concrete block post. Its radiator and starting handle projected at the other end. (S.W. Baker)

49. The new block post replaced the two earlier ones and can be seen to have 45 levers. The two lines at the bottom right of the diagram connect with Woolmer and the two at

the top left with Longmoor Yard. One of the latter had to be removed to meet MOT requirements at the B2131 road crossing. (Lens of Sutton)

50. One of the attractions at the 1949 open day (and subsequently) was *Gazelle*, a diminutive 0–4–2WT reputed to be the smallest standard gauge locomotive built. Its story is long and devious – its association with the Army accidental and unusual. It is worth a visit to the Museum of Army Transport to see it now. (Lens of Sutton)

51. Each annual open day drew great crowds. This is 1955, with 0–6–0ST no. 11 *Brussels* leaving for Liss and exhibit no. 4 the old Dean Goods being rerailed for th umpteenth time. *Brussels* was to be foun subsequently nearby at the Hollycomb Steam Collection at Liphook, but in 1971 was moved to the Keighley & Worth Valle Railway. (R.C. Riley collection)

52. The 1965 event is illustrated by Ruston diesel no. 8227 *Hassan* and Hunslet 0–6–0ST no. 195. A bridge-building exercise was another popular subject to observe, particularly when a *train* of several 2–10–0s rumbled over it at the end of the day. (E. Wilmshurst)

53. The circuit of the Hollywater Loop on the open day on 30th April 1966 was undertaken in brake vans, hauled by 0–6–0 diesel no. 878 *Basra*. This machine had been built in 1945 by English Electric for the LMS. (S.W. Baker)

4. The 1967 open day was held on 3rd June ut the northern limit of passenger operation as, by then, Oakhanger. Hunslet no. D199 accelerates the 14.00 departure westards. (J.H. Bird)

55. Snow falls and press cameras flash as Major General Errol Lonsdale unveils the plate bearing his name on Hunslet 0–6–0ST no. AD196 on 7th January 1968. The locomotive now earns its keep on the steep gradients of the Mid-Hants Railway. (J.H. Bird)

5. Early in 1968 hopes were high for the establishment of a railway preservation centre at Longmoor. Five ex-BR engines were stored there when one of them, David Shepherd's class 9F no. 92203, went to Liss to haul the Bulleid Pacific Preservation Society's special train to Longmoor. On arrival, it was named *Black Prince* by Major General Lonsdale. The date was 8th June. (J.A.M. Vaughan)

7. ARMY 777 was a 1959 BR conversion (S7921S) of a Maunsell 8ft wide Hastings line Brake Second (SR4444) which arrived at Longmoor in 1968 and was one of the last 'new' vehicles to be acquired. BR converted four coaches to ambulance ward cars for Lourdes pilgrims and this represents perhaps the last word in comfort in coaches of this type. It made an interesting exhibit at the penultimate open day on 28th September 1968. (G.M. Moon)

58. The railway's administrative headquarters was south of the main road and Longmoor Downs station. For many years *Gazelle* and *Woolmer* were exhibited between it and the parade ground. (J. Scrace)

59. Civilian employees undertook a variety of tasks from door handle cleaning to driving. This ex-SECR Birdcage coach is displaying both vacuum and air brake connections. (J.A.M. Vaughan)

60. A record crowd of over 10,000 peop appeared for the last open day on 5th Ju 1969. Many of them lined the platform to wi ness the use of ramp wagon no. WD4204 These wagons were fitted with jacks and removable wheel set. Their purpose is re ealed in the next photograph. (G.M. Moor

61. With only one wheel set in place, the wagon could be used to load or unload tanks at any location – a few sleepers were generally laid between the running rails. Note the buffer hinged out of the path of the tank tracks. (G.M. Moon)

62. Army railway resources were much reduced by the time of the last open day and so this passenger train had been augmented with two coaches from the Army Depot at Bicester. No. 600 *Gordon* prepares for another trip to Liss, having earlier in the day hauled a nine-coach enthusiasts' special from the main BR line. (J.A.M. Vaughan)

63. Public Days, as they were originally called, were held annually from 1947, with the exception of 1951 and 1952. *Gordon* makes one of its last public runs on 5th July 1969, returning from Liss. On the right is the line to Longmoor Yard, the signal school also being visible. (D. Fereday Glenn)

64. Formal closure took place with a ceremony on the platform on 31st October 1969, total closure occurring on 31st January 1970. Trains departed simultaneously at 14.45 for Oakhanger and Liss, both returning within two minutes of 15.20. (J.A.M. Vaughan)

LONGMOOR LEVEL CROSSINGS

65. The sign makes clear the number of crossings to be encountered, although the western one was double track and could cause confusion. Road users were often presented with a fine view of current military equipment. (Museum of Army Transport)

66. A WWII photograph shows a trai bound for Liss, the double track crossing t the yard being behind the Army lorry. Eas wards, behind the camera, a further crossin linked the yard with the Hollywater Loop. (H.N. James)

67. Looking in the same direction as the previous photograph, but on 30th June 1967, we witness the guard switching on the flashing warning lights to protect road users, before Hunslet 0–6–0ST no. 195 proceeds towards Liss. The station and yard crossing are more obvious in this view. (D. Fereday Glenn)

68. In April 1968, there were still some lengthy trains to delay traffic on the otherwise straight, fast road. Ruston no. 8219 throbs gently over the highway, as the two-armed signal remains off. (D. Fereday Glenn)

69. Belt and braces – the flashing red lights and the traditional red flag are in use on 7th January 1969, as no. AD878 *Basra* descends into the yard, past the signal school. (J.H. Bird)

LONGMOOR BRIDGE

70. This is the first span to be erected over the approach to Longmoor Yard and was 100ft long. It had been recovered from Hopkins Bridge site, on the north side of the Hollywater Loop, in the 1920s.
(E.R. Lacey collection)

71. A 1938 view shows 0–6–2T *Gordon* arriving from Liss, with Weavers Down rising to over 500ft in the background. The bridge was unsuccessfully bombed by German planes during WWII, as it was believed to carry the main line to Portsmouth.
(National Railway Museum)

72. No. 6 bridge was replaced by a span of 110ft in 1952. No. 195 is seen crossing it at about 05.30 on 30th June 1967, with an empty coach to form the first up staff train from Liss. The vehicle below is an ex-Nord van used for tools. It is thought to have been brought back from France in 1940.
(D. Fereday Glenn)

3. The yard makes an ideal place to view o.600 *Gordon*, as it arrives with the 18.30 om Liss on 5th July 1969. Other long lost features are the diesel filler on the left and the permanent way hut on the right. (S.C. Nash)

LONGMOOR YARD

4. A 1931 view from the bridge shows, from ft to right, the power station; stores; work-1ops; lifting shed (the tall building in line ith the fence); boiler shop; running shed; coal stage; IC engine shed; carriage shed (behind the steam) and the mobilisation stores. (Museum of Army Transport)

75. Few places in Britain could offer sight of such a diverse collection of rolling stock. We offer a small selection. Firstly, an ex-GWR machine, built in 1890 as an 0–4–2T and which was in use on the WIMR from about 1908 to 1921. It had a rigid wheelbase – the rear wheels were not bogies. (Lens of Sutton)

76. *Thisbe* was built in 1911 by Hawthorn Leslie to the design of H.F. Stephens, later better known as manager of a large assortment of light railways. It was bought from the Shropshire and Montgomeryshire Railway by the WD and appears to have run on the WIMR between about 1916 and 1931. (Pamlin Prints)

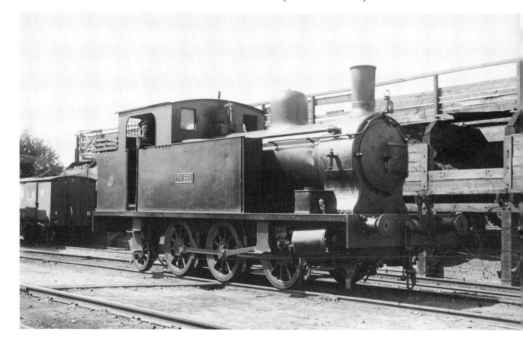

7. This 1919 60cm gauge Hunslet arrived in
)34, as an instructional model, being scrap-
ed in 1961. In 1986, the Chalk Pits Museum
: Amberley rescued a similar locomotive
om India, at considerable expense!
G. Alliez/R.C. Riley collection)

78. Hudswell Clarke & Co built this 4–4–0T
in 1880. It ran on the M&GNJR and eventually on the WIMR from 1915 until 1930, bearing the name *Kingsley*. Thereafter, it was
used for rerailing practice until being cut up
in 1952. The light patches are gas detector
paint. (H.N. James)

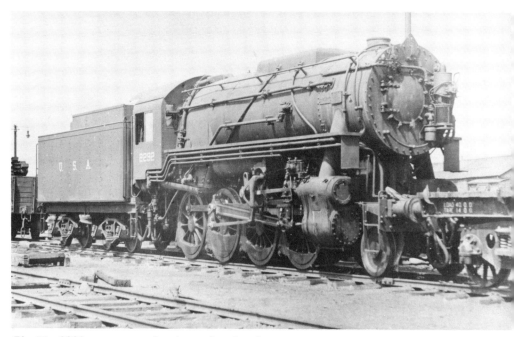

79. No. 2292 was one of a large batch of 2–8–0s built in the USA for the European campaign, this example appearing at Longmoor in about 1943. Many similar engines were to run on the railways of Britain, although devoid of the ugly air compressor on the front. (R.C. Riley collection)

80. About 15 USA Whitcombe diesel electric Bo-Bo locomotives were present on the line in 1944 and two were retained in regular service until the mid-1950s. It is the camp sewage works that is out of bound to troops (R.C. Riley)

81. Gipsy Hollow was the name given to an extensive range of storage sidings east of the yard. For a period it was connected to the Hollywater Loop by a line over the B2131. This June 1948 photograph shows part of a vast quantity of Austerity 2–10–0s awaiting disposal after the hostilities. (S.W. Baker)

82. Large numbers of Austerity 0–6–0s were stored for some time. Many later found a second career serving British industry, whilst a relatively small number were retained by the Army. (H.C. Casserley)

83. Another 1948 view shows part of the 75cm gauge track on which ran two Wehrmacht Gmeinder diesels captured from the Germans, who had reputably used them at the notorious V2 rocket sites at Peenemunde. Until 1957, they were operated for diesel hydraulic instructional purposes, on what was known as the Weavers Down Light Railway. (S.W. Baker)

84. We see rerailing operations in sever. photographs in this album. This is the trai that, in 1948, carried all the necessary equip ment, which included jacks, ramps, packin and slings. The jack van was an ex-RO} mobile compressor van and the vehicl beyond it is reputed to have once served as a East Coast Joint Stock sleeping car. (S.W. Baker)

85. This locomotive was on loan to the NER in 1944 when the munitions train it was hauling exploded at Soham on 2nd June. After extensive repairs by its maker, North British Locomotive Co., it served in Europe and returned to Longmoor where it is seen on 1st August 1963. (G.M. Moon)

86. A view of the running shed on 2nd September 1964 shows, from left to right, 0–6–0ST no. 157 *Constantine*, 2–10–0 no. 601 *Kitchener* (3), 0–6–0ST no. 156 *Tobruk* and 2–10–0 no. 400 *Sir Guy Williams*. The building on the right is the diesel fitting shed, which included a ground level wheel lathe. (G.M. Moon)

87. One of the popular "blue saloons" was this ex-LNWR inspection vehicle, from the Webb era. It survived in the hands of the Transport Trust and after many years of open storage on the Severn Valley Railway, it is now to be found on the Kent & East Sussex Railway. The building in the background housed the signal school on the upper floor, operations control being on the ground floor. (E. Wilmshurst)

88. No. AD156 was renamed *McMurdo* an is seen on 30th April 1966 alongside the lif ing shop. On the right is the paint shop – th diesel shed and school is behind the breal down crane, a Ransomes Rapier 45 ton. (S.W. Baker)

89. In 1967, the diesel school used Fowler 0–4–0 no. 17 for instructional purposes. It had been built in 1940, with works no. 22912, but never ran on the LMR, being ex-Royal Ordnance Factory. The components on stands were for teaching purposes. (G.M. Moon)

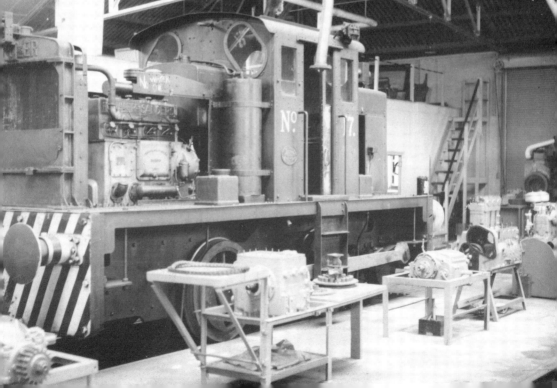

90. On 8th June 1968, the view from no. 6 bridge included a number of locomotives that were forming the nucleus of the proposed preservation centre. In steam is West Country class no. 34023 *Blackmore Vale*. A

notable addition to the buildings in about 1951 is the long carriage shed, partly obscured by steam, that was formerly the ambulance train shed at Netley Hospital. (J. Scrace)

1. A rebuilt Bulleid Pacific was also resident at Longmoor in 1968. No. 35028 *Clan Line* was receiving the attention of the photographers on 28th September, in the company of *Black Prince*. In 1987, *Clan Line* resided at Southall, between spells of duty on steam services from Marylebone. (J. Scrace)

WEAVERS DOWN

3. On 1st May 1965, a demonstration armed train was run. It carried a crew of 30 men and sufficient tools and permanent way material to repair any track damage caused by the detonation of explosives by the leading bogie. (E. Wilmshurst)

2. Other preserved locomotives residing at Longmoor in 1968 included David Shepherd's BR Standard class 4 and *Lord Fisher*, a 1915 Barclay product. Both are now at the East Somerset Railway, the former bearing the name *The Green Knight*. The Army presence was much reduced by then, evidenced by the weeds near the "antifreeze" stove. (J.H. Bird)

94. By the 28th September 1968, the scene was one of dereliction. The once busy passing loop had long been clipped and padlocked, the levers having been moved into the open. No. AD196 speeds towards Liss on another enjoyable open day. (J.A.M. Vaughan)

```
LONGMOOR MILITARY RAILWAY STATISTICS
          1 NOV 68 - 31 OCT 69


No of passenger trains run   -   2,830
No of passenger train miles  -  12,735
No of passengers carried     -  53,642
No of goods and spl trains   -     209
No of goods and spl miles    -   2,610
Total train miles            -   3,039
Total miles                  -  15,345
```

95. One of the most spectacular trains to run in peacetime was seen on the last open day, 5th July 1969. AD no. 600 glides along with steam to spare with the five AD coaches seen in picture no. 62, to which had been added nine BR coaches from Waterloo. (J. Scrace)

LISS FOREST ROAD

96. Work on the Liss extension started at Longmoor in about 1924. This photograph, from March 1933, shows the Army's Cowans Sheldon steam shovel at work, creating a cutting near Liss Forest Road. (Museum of Army Transport)

7. It appears that the Army undertook the entire construction work, using its own manpower and machines. The latter included a pile driver, seen here preparing for the crossing of the River Rother, west of the station, which is in the distance. (Museum of Army Transport)

98. Sappers are noted for ingenuity and it is exemplified in the boom track layer, which passed materials ahead of the construction train. It was used during the building of the Liss extension and was later restricted to the Hollywater Loop, as it grossly exceeded the loading gauge.
(Museum of Army Transport)

9. The boiler and engine were from a York-hire steam wagon and the winches were of narine origin. Looking towards the rear of ne train, we see some sleepers from the rear vagons travelling along the left conveyor. The exposed shafting and gears are worth lose examination. (Museum of Army Transport)

100. Looking towards Liss, soon after the opening, the unusual catch siding is evident on the right. It was 240 yards long. Its sharp curve and terminal sand drag were apparently intended to bring errant train crews to a gentle halt. (Museum of Army Transport)

101. A picture in the opposite direction completes the view of the last station on Army property. The acquisition of land for the remainder of the line was a protracted business and the first indication that SR officials had of the coming railway was surveyor's marker posts near their boundary fence. (Museum of Army Transport)

103. The coach was first drawn away by a sister engine, no. 7362, which then fetched the rerailing vans, whilst onlookers rested on the embankment. These engines were immediately suited to LMR requirements as they were air braked, being of GER origin. In 1956, the only serious accident on the line took place near here, resulting in six fatalities. (H.N. James)

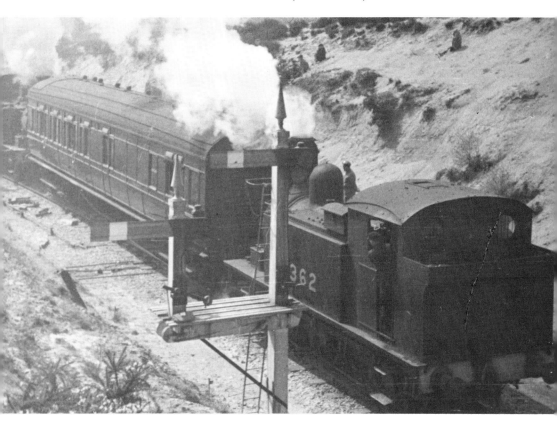

102. Accidents are inevitable on a training railway. This one, during WWII, was attributed to the mis-reading of signals. The victim is LNER class J69 0–6–0T no. 7056. (H.N. James)

London & South Western Ry.
This Ticket is issued subject to the Regulations & Conditions stated in the Company's Time Tables & Bills

5th Btn. County of London Regt.
LONDON to
LIPHOOK
THIRD CLASS
July 28th to Aug. 15th 1910

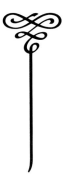

104. Embankment on-lookers had an entirely different scene to witness on the 1986 open day. Ruston Hornsby diesel hydraulic no. 8219 (re-numbered 425 that year) arrives with passengers from Longmoor whilst no. 890 (later 610) 0–8–0 *General Lord Robertson* waits to pass with modern civil engineering equipment. (J.H. Bird)

105. Another view of the spectacular 14-coach train on the final open day shows almost its entire length. It is seen arriving from Liss, again with spare steam. The locomotive's dual braking system continues to be of value on the Severn Valley Railway, where it h hauled air-braked ballast trains from BR well as the regular vacuum braked passeng trains. Note the buffer stops, high on the le (J.A.M. Vaughan)

S.R. L.W.D.S.O., WOKING.   D.C.73 LWD.   16TH APRIL, 1943.

D I V I S I O N A L   · C I R C U L A R.

(1) LISS. CONNECTION WITH LONGMOOR MILITARY RAILWAY.
       Referring to the alterations which are to be carried out on Sunday 18th April, and which are referred to in Signalling Instruction No. 11, 1943, all concerned to note that S.R. engines may proceed over the four Military Loop Sidings and the Longmoor Military Railway Shunting Neck which has been provided in connection therewith.
                                                   A.1/6479.
                          ----

(2) STOVE VAN NO. 421.
       One fire bucket, which has the word "Van and No. 421" painted on the side is missing. Any station having this article on hand should send it to C.M.E. Clapham Junction.   A.4/-

                          ----

(3) WOODEN ROLLERS FOR TOILET ROLLS.
       As the supply of toilet rolls to stations has ceased, Station Masters to arrange the removal of the wooden rollers and have them placed in safe custody until after the war.   A.456.

)6. The first through troop train from the ain line is composed of ten coaches and two ns hauled by a USA built Austerity. The original LMR line to the terminus is in the foreground. (Museum of Army Transport)

In 1942 exchange sidings were laid down d connection made with the SR *for use in emergency*, should the necessity arise. The ar Office would not authorise the cost of gnalling the connection and so the Long-oor authorities made a local arrangement hereby the Drewry railcar would enter the R goods shed to fetch items when required. n 30th November 1942, consent was given r up to four wagons per day to be transfer-d in this way! SR engines were forbidden to enter the WD sidings, as they were unbal-lasted. Eventualy, the War Office authorised £1182 for the signalling; the SR provided 500 cu.yds. of ash in lieu of ballast and the con-nection was brought into use on 18th April 1943. This 1970 edition shows the link, although the local goods yard tracks had been lifted. These are shown on earlier maps which are to be found under pictures 71 and 72 in our *Woking to Portsmouth* album.

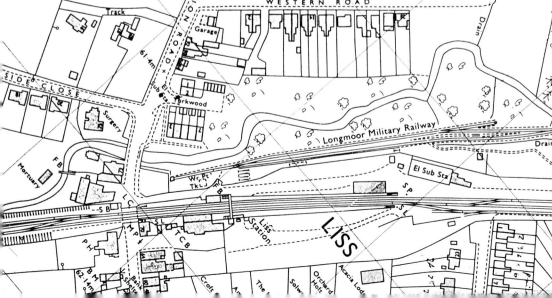

107. A block post was provided at the junction, which was ½ mile from the end of the line. The points are under the leading coach of the 1.14 Liss to Oakhanger, seen here on 28th September 1968, headed by Hunslet no. 196 *Errol Lonsdale*. (S.C. Nash)

108. Looking north from inside the boundary gate with BR, the overgrown tracks still displayed their original ash ballast, long after closure. Most of the coaches and wagons were sold for preservation, the last few are seen here awaiting dispersal. Until about 1950 access to all four roads had been possible from this end.
(Museum of Army Transport)

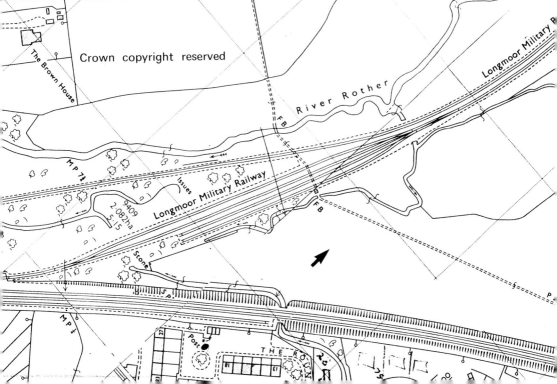

109. A view of the terminus soon after its opening in August 1933 includes the block post and the SR goods shed. The buffer stops were not surprisingly replaced by a very substantial concrete block which remained for years after the closure of the railway. (Museum of Army Transport)

110. A closer look at the end of the line eight miles from Bordon, shows its relationship to SR up platform shelter on the left. The signal box is in the distance and the tall down starting signal is also visible. (Museum of Army Transport)

111. A photograph from the SR footbridge on 17th May 1934 shows the Hawthorn Leslie 0–6–0T *Selborne* and the end of one of two sidings in the up goods yard. No shelter was provided for passengers at that time – adequate clothing had already been issued. (H.C. Casserley)

112. Three Adams Jubilee class A12 0–4–2s were hired from the SR in the middle of WWII. After the failure of the scheme to establish the proposed Historic Transport Centre at Longmoor, the land seen in this photograph was fenced in. Eight locomotives were stored here in 1970-71. (H.N. James)

113. A northward panorama from the station footbridge in June 1948 shows a waiting shelter on the left. Hundreds of servicemen changed trains here at weekends at that time. On the right is the junction signal for the connecting line. (S.W. Baker)

LONGMOOR
OAKHANGER or BORDON

TIME		DESTINATION	REMARKS
0650	Daily to	LONGMOOR	SUNDAYS EXCEPTED
0715	" "	BORDON	" "
0750	" "	LONGMOOR	" "
0845	" "	" "	
1045	" "	" "	
1145	" "	" "	SUNDAYS EXCEPTED
1245	" "	" "	" "
1345	" "	" "	
1445	" "	" "	SUNDAYS EXCEPTED
1715	" "	OAKHANGER	SATS. & SUN "
1745	" "	LONGMOOR	SUNDAYS EXCEPTED
1845	" "	" "	
1945	" "	" "	SUNDAYS EXCEPTED
2115		" "	SUNDAYS ONLY
2215	" "	" "	
23.5	" "	" "	TO BORDON. SUN. ONLY

114. The 1948 departure board shows two extra trains on Sunday evening for those returning from leave. (S.W. Baker)

115. Not all derailments were intentional.
o. 195 helps to pull no. 196 back onto the
ad on 3rd June 1967. The witnesses are sil-
houetted against the concrete block men-
oned earlier. (G.M. Moon)

116. The equipment employed was the time
honoured rerailing ramp. Rebellious wagons
could often be retrained in a matter of minutes using this method. (G.M. Moon)

117. The Wickham type 40 mk.IIA inspection car arrived from Bicester in 1960 and saw regular service until the end of the line. The platform slabs here and at Longmoor Downs were SR products. (J.A.M. Vaughan)

118. On 1st July 1968, the service was operated by 36 ton Ruston Hornsby 0–6–0 *Hassan*. Driving instructors frequently drew the attention of their pupils to the fact that the building in the distance was occupied by the local undertaker! The water tank, beyond the shelter, was dismantled long after closure, for re-use on the Mid-Hants Railway. (J.H. Bird)

L.M.R.   L.M.R.

JULY 5th 1969

COMMEMORATIVE TICKET ISSUED TO MARK THE
LONGMOOR/BORDON GARRISON OPEN DAY

CONDITIONS

THIS TICKET DOES NOT CONSTITUTE A RIGHT OF ACCESS
TO TRAINS OR PROPERTY ON THE LMR NOR IS IT
REQUIRED FOR TRAVEL ON TRAINS OF THE LMR

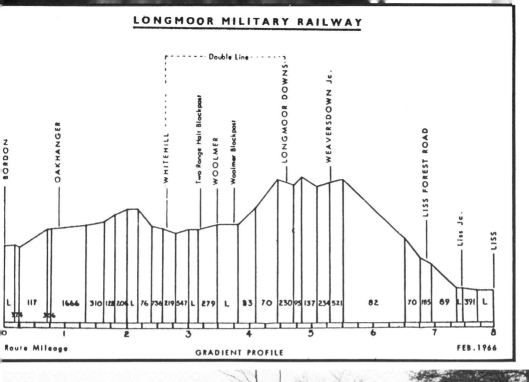

LONGMOOR MILITARY RAILWAY

Double Line

BORDON — OAKHANGER — WHITEHILL — Two Range Halt Blockpost — WOOLMER — Woolmer Blockpost — LONGMOOR DOWNS — WEAVERSDOWN Jc. — LISS FOREST ROAD — Liss Jc. — LISS

Route Mileage

GRADIENT PROFILE

FEB. 1966

119. 1968 saw the arrival of David Shepherd's class 4 4–6–0 no. 75029 under its own steam from Cricklewood. An Army flagman stands in the track at his boundary, the gate now being obscured by the engine. (J.H. Bird)

120. The nine coaches of one of the mos memorable trains to run on the line are seer arriving for the final exhilerating open day o 5th July 1969. The train ran from Waterloo vi Staines, Reading, Basingstoke and Eastleigh What a marvellous way to spend 32/6 o £1.62½, even if earlier you had been *paid* to work on the LMR. (J.H. Bird)

THE MUSEUM
OF ARMY TRANSPORT

MUSEUM OF ARMY TRANSPORT
Flemingate, Beverley,
North Humberside HU17 0NG

Entertaining, enlightening and educating, there is nothing like it in the Country. In this two-acre hall you will find the Army Railway Museum, dozens of vehicles in exciting settings, from a field workshop to an amphibious assault landing, and a light aircraft. The display includes the wagon used by Lord Roberts in the Boer War, the Rolls Royce used by Field Marshal Montgomery in World War II and the only three-wheels-in-a-row motor cycle.

In the railway section you will find the only rail destroyer in captivity, six small locomotives and some tank carrying wagons. The Museum provides excitement for veterans, enthusiasts and children alike.

Large car park, a well stocked shop and "Cookhouse".
Open: Daily 10.00 a.m. to 5.00 p.m. **All year round.**

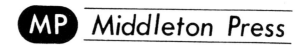

MP Middleton Press

Easebourne Lane, Midhurst, West Sussex, GU29 9AZ
☎ Midhurst (073 081) 3169

BRANCH LINES

BRANCH LINES TO MIDHURST	0 906520 01 0
BRANCH LINES TO HORSHAM	0 906520 02 9
BRANCH LINE TO SELSEY	0 906520 04 5
BRANCH LINES TO EAST GRINSTEAD	0 906520 07 X
BRANCH LINES TO ALTON	0 906520 11 8
BRANCH LINE TO HAYLING	0 906520 12 6
BRANCH LINE TO SOUTHWOLD	0 906520 15 0
BRANCH LINE TO TENTERDEN	0 906520 21 5
BRANCH LINES TO NEWPORT	0 906520 26 6
BRANCH LINES TO TUNBRIDGE WELLS	0 906520 32 0
BRANCH LINE TO SWANAGE	0 906520 33 9
BRANCH LINES AROUND GOSPORT	0 906520 36 3
BRANCH LINES TO LONGMOOR	0 906520 41 X

SOUTH COAST RAILWAYS

BRIGHTON TO WORTHING	0 906520 03 7
WORTHING TO CHICHESTER	0 906520 06 1
CHICHESTER TO PORTSMOUTH	0 906520 14 2
BRIGHTON TO EASTBOURNE	0 906520 16 9
RYDE TO VENTNOR	0 906520 19 3
EASTBOURNE TO HASTINGS	0 906520 27 4
PORTSMOUTH TO SOUTHAMPTON	0 906520 31 2
HASTINGS TO ASHFORD	0 906520 37 1
SOUTHAMPTON TO BOURNEMOUTH	0 906520 42 8

SOUTHERN MAIN LINES

WOKING TO PORTSMOUTH	0 906520 25 8
HAYWARDS HEATH TO SEAFORD	0 906520 28 2
EPSOM TO HORSHAM	0 906520 30 4
CRAWLEY TO LITTLEHAMPTON	0 906520 34 7
THREE BRIDGES TO BRIGHTON	0 906520 35 5
WATERLOO TO WOKING	0 906520 38 X
VICTORIA TO EAST CROYDON	0 906520 40 1

STEAMING THROUGH

STEAMING THROUGH KENT	0 906520 13 4
STEAMING THROUGH EAST HANTS	0 906520 18 5
STEAMING THROUGH EAST SUSSEX	0 906520 22 3
STEAMING THROUGH SURREY	0 906520 39 8

OTHER RAILWAY BOOKS

WAR ON THE LINE The official history of the SR in World War II	0 906520 10 X
GARRAWAY FATHER AND SON The story of two careers in steam	0 906520 20 7

OTHER BOOKS

MIDHURST TOWN – THEN & NOW	0 906520 05 3
EAST GRINSTEAD – THEN & NOW	0 906520 17 7
THE MILITARY DEFENCE OF WEST SUSSEX	0 906520 23 1
WEST SUSSEX WATERWAYS	0 906520 24 X
BATTLE OVER PORTSMOUTH A City at war in 1940	0 906520 29 0